Come Home

A gifted spiritual director and teacher by example, Sr. Marie Schwan writes an eminently practical and readily accessible book on living from one's center. In true Ignatian style, she reminds us that the door is everywhere, the way is Jesus, and the maps—though rooted in Christian tradition—are also shaped by one's own particular personality, history, and gifts.

Cynthia Sabathier, C.S.J.
Director, St. Joseph Spirituality Center

Marie Schwan, C.S.J., brings to this slim yet potent text years of experience in spiritual direction and retreat work. Enriching and challenging, *Come Home* is a call to live at the center, rather than the circumference, of our lives.

Bishop Robert F. Morneau
Auxiliary Bishop of Green Bay

Marie Schwan's vivid and often poignant reflections synthesize the best of today's spirituality and give practical advice for handling life's woundedness and coming home to our center within. Perfect reading for Christians seeking to abide more fully in God.

Richard Hauser, S.J.
Director of the Master's Program in Christian Spirituality
Creighton University

Come Home

A Prayer Journey

to the

Center Within

MARIE SCHWAN, C.S.J.

ave maria press notre dame, indiana

Founded in 1865, Ave Maria Press is a ministry of the Indiana Province of Holy Cross.

www.avemariapress.com

ISBN-10 1-59471-229-8   ISBN-13 978-1-59471-229-6

Cover image ©corbis images

Interior art © Jupiter Images

Cover and text design by Brian C. Conley

Printed and bound in the United States of America.

Library of Congress Cataloging-in-Publication Data
    Schwan, Marie.
      Come home : a prayer journey to the center within / Marie Schwan.
        p. cm.
      Includes bibliographical references.
      ISBN-13: 978-1-59471-229-6 (pbk.)
      ISBN-10: 1-59471-229-8 (pbk.)
      1. Prayer--Christianity. I. Title.
      BV210.3.S39 2010
      248.3'2--dc22

                                    2009043935

Contents

Introduction

The Sunday after Katrina devastated New Orleans, I found myself at a midmorning Mass in Baton Rouge. Along with my sisters, I had left New Orleans mere hours before the hurricane was scheduled to hit land. We had each left with a small suitcase, expecting, as in the past, to return within a few days. A week later, we knew the devastation that had struck the city: the flooding, the people who fled, the people who were holed up in the dome under incredibly painful, even gruesome conditions.

Along with my sisters, I was one of the fortunate ones who found shelter, and was assured of a place to live, food, a future. But that morning as I prepared for Mass, I was suddenly aware of how foreign it all seemed. I was in a church, magnificent in architecture, but somehow forbidding, listening to a choir sing unfamiliar hymns, witnessing people whom I did not know greeting each other like long-lost friends. And in the midst of it all, I experienced a wave of grief, of pain, of aloneness that burst up from my depths with the thought, "I just want to go home." And then, the realization that home was no more.

I reprimanded myself. I am a member of a religious community that assures me that I will always be cared for; I have friends and family members. Was I merely feeling sorry for the loss of things that were easily replaceable?

Then, it occurred to me that what I was experiencing was not only my grief, but the grief of all those people in the dome, those still stranded on the overpasses, those who did not know where family members might be, or even if they were still alive. The grief of the people washed over me.

The following morning, during my time of prayer, I began to journal about my experience, and from the tip of my pen flowed the words, "O God, your other name is Home."

Our God is a God who calls us home to that place within us that is at once our own heart and God's own dwelling. Our God yearns for us. We hear this in the story of the prodigal son where Jesus tells us about the father who waited for the return of his son (Luke 15). We see this yearning spelled out in the way that the father rushes out to meet the son when he sees him on the road. We see it in the way he embraces the son, ragged, dirty, smelling like the pigpen in which he has been working. The father invites him to come home, draws him back into the household, restoring him to sonship.

The parable came to life for me in the story of a woman I know whose son disappeared for many months, stretching even into a year or more. She grieved for him, prayed, and trusted that one day she would hear from him. Finally one evening, the phone rang. She answered it. She heard a tentative, "Mom." "Where are you?" she cried, "Come home."

"Mom, I'm in California."

"Do you need a ticket? I'll send you money. Just come home."

"Mom, I'm gay."

"That's ok. Come home."

"But mom, I'm HIV positive."

The woman said that just for a fraction of a moment she hesitated. This was in the early '90s when the fear of the contagion of AIDS was rampant, and hospitals were sometimes hesitant to take patients with AIDS. Then, she said, "You come home; we love you and we'll take care of you."

Like the father in the parable, like this caring mother, God says to each of us, "Come home."

This is a book about coming home to that deep place within us where God dwells. I like to think of it as a guide to embracing the wonder of God's presence within us, and as a help to maintain and return to that center.

While it is not primarily a book on centering prayer, it does embrace the concepts that underlie centering prayer. Like so many others, I too owe a debt of gratitude to Frs.

Thomas Keating, Basil Pennington, and Thomas Merton who have called us back to our contemplative roots.

I want to thank the many people who have been a part of helping me to plumb some of the depths of this mystery. I am grateful to my community, the Sisters of St. Joseph, who have supported my journey. I want to thank the Jesuits who have fostered my spiritual development through retreats, spiritual direction, and also have invited me to collaborate in their ministry. I want to thank family and friends for their love. And in a special way, I want to thank the retreatants, many of them part of Twelve Step programs. They have contributed to the development of the ideas in this book by listening, sharing, and encouraging me in the writing of it.

one

The Center Within

"Martha, Martha, you worry and fret about so many things, and yet few are needed, indeed only one."

—Luke 10:41

What is the one thing needed? The one thing necessary? What is it that keeps you going? What is it that gives your life meaning?

In the midst of this busy, driven world, filled with broken promises, how do you keep your balance? What helps you walk with integrity in the midst of the chaos?

Whatever it is—this one thing—it affects not only your understanding of yourself, but also your understanding of and relationship with God, with each other person in your life, and even with your relationship with material things.

In the gospel, Mary was commended by Jesus because she had chosen the one thing necessary. She sat at the feet of Jesus, in the pose and place of the disciple, and listened. We, too, are invited to be still and to listen deeply.

We enter into a stillness within so that we can come home to that deep place within us where our God dwells, to that place where we not only meet God, but are connected to every other created reality.

So, we are invited to consider that each of us has a deep place where we are most who we are. In that place we know ourselves as true, good, and beautiful. That truth and goodness and beauty were affirmed by those who have loved us. "You are *my* precious little boy/girl." "I am so proud of you." "You are so gifted." "You are always so caring." Words like these—even the memory of them—continue to affirm that central place.

And apart from someone else's words, there are moments when we tap into this center. It may be in the presence of a magnificent sunset, or the far reaches of a starry sky on a dark night. It may be in the arms of someone who loves us, or in the moment of holding a newborn child. It may be an unexpected experience of profound prayer, or an insight that comes unbidden.

In that moment, we *know* "the one thing necessary."

In the experience, when we are in touch with that center of truth and goodness and beauty, we relate to God, to self, to others, to things with what can be called harmony, wholeness, cleanness, serenity. From that place the "Spirit cries out 'Abba'" (Rom 8:15).

Experiences of centeredness such as these become an indelible part of the soul. They remain, to be recalled at will. These experiences become for us what the burning bush and the Exodus are for the People of God—moments and memories in which God is somehow always accessible to us, and we to God.

For your consideration and prayerful reflection:

- Prayerfully read and reread Luke 10:38–42. Imagine yourself sitting at the feet of Jesus. Enter into a profound quiet. Simply be there. Be aware of your feelings and any images that arise to your memory or imagination.

- Recall and list times when your have experienced being centered. After you have listed them, prayerfully enter into and recreate one of them: the people involved, the scene, kind of day, etc. Consider how it has shaped your life. In that moment, what was your relationship to yourself, to God, to others, to things?

- Make the following your own:

  > In returning and rest you shall be saved; in quietness and in trust shall be your strength. (Is 30:15 NRSV)

two

When We Are Centered

Enough for me to keep my soul
tranquil and quiet
like a child in its mother's arms,
as content as a child that has been
weaned.

—Psalm 131:2

What is life like for you when you are centered?

Think of people you know who live their lives with a certain contentment and peacefulness. Think of how attractive such a life is. It does not mean that they do not struggle or that they do not have painful situations with which to cope, yet there is a quality of life that is most attractive.

11

What do you notice about them?

It seems to me that there is a harmony in their lives. The parts of their lives seem to fit together like the pieces of a puzzle, revealing the truth, the beauty, the goodness that is at the heart of each person. We notice a joyfulness and a freedom that quickly brings a smile, or even tears to their eyes. They generously do what another may need of them.

So what will it mean for us if we move toward living a centered life?

In relationship to God: Insofar as we are truly centered, our image of God will be one that Jesus reveals to us, of a God who is loving and forgiving, a God who nurtures and heals and is always looking to set us free. The God that we know and who shapes our lives will be one to whom we are personally related and in whom we put our total trust.

Our desire for centeredness will lead us to the liturgies that are the celebration of our Christian tradition. Through participation our hearts are nourished with word and ritual. We are part of something bigger than ourselves. Hopefully, we are drawn to make our own the prayers that have shaped generations before us, and we will be led to growth in our own spontaneous and personal reflection, speaking to God in our own words, and listening for God's response.

It is essential that we give time to this most precious of relationships, that is, our relationship with God, just as we give time to any relationship that is important to us. It will mean a daily and regular time spent in quality prayer. It will mean honoring the Sabbath day that is a precious part of our Judeo/Christian tradition. Contrary to so much of our societal compulsiveness, the Sabbath is meant for prayer, for rest, for play. For the Jewish people, it is a day of leisure in a world where only the nobility had leisure. The Sabbath was a sign of being a child of the Most High. It was a sign of the Covenant. One rabbi suggested that if all of Israel kept one Sabbath holy, the kingdom would come!

When we make time for the people and things we love, that loving use of time is a sign of the level of centeredness out of which we shape our lives.

In relationship to self: When we are centered, we have a healthy, honest, grateful sense of well-being. We know our gifts and we stand tall in them. We are self-nurturing, self-directed, finding and making use of what we authentically need for our ongoing journey toward maturity. When we are centered, we have a resilience and a playfulness and a healthy attitude toward the work that we do. We say yes to the gift of who we are.

In relationship to others: When we are centered, we are separate but mutual, having boundaries that are flexible. We can be both affirming and challenging, but always with compassion and a courteous reverence. The caring, nurturing, freeing, healing attributes of our God—revealed in Jesus— are lived out in our love for each of the others who are part of the network of relationships that makes up our lives.

In relationship to things: When we are centered, we have a great love and appreciation for all of creation, for all the things that are part of our human existence. Our love for things is ordered so that we use them, but do not abuse them. We experience ourselves as having what we need, and we can be generous in sharing with others who may be in need.

In his letter to the Galatians, St. Paul calls the community to a freedom that can only come from a deep centeredness. He says:

> When Christ freed us, he meant us to remain free. Stand firm, therefore, and do not submit again to the yoke of slavery. . . . Let me put it this way, if you are guided by the Spirit you will be in no danger of yielding to self-indulgence. . . . What the spirit brings is . . . love, joy, peace, patience, kindness, goodness, trustfulness, gentleness and self-control. (Gal 5:1, 16, 22)

For your consideration and prayerful reflection:

- Reread this chapter, using it as an examination of how you live out of your own center, perhaps not always perfectly or consistently, but at least in desire. With which descriptive phrases do you most identify? Thank God for each of them, and ask to be strengthened in them.

- Prayerfully reread Galatians 5:1, 16, 22. How do Paul's words speak to your heart, to what you want your life to be?

- Pray Psalm 131.

three

Pulled Off Center

We are only the earthenware jars that
hold this treasure, to make it clear that
such an overwhelming power comes
from God and not from us.

—2 Corinthians 4:7

We may be true, good, and beautiful. There are indelible moments when we experience ourselves in this way, but it is not easy for us to stay in these moments; that is, to live our lives from this center. When Paul speaks of the human condition, he speaks of sin, and his word for sin means "to miss the mark." If ever you have attempted archery, or even darts, you know the skill it takes to always hit the bull's-eye!

In life, too, we often miss the mark. We slip into being bitter or critical, and we may find ourselves holding a grudge. Or we may be so over-focused on something like dieting, or our own self-importance and popularity, that we lose awareness of others. Our off-centeredness may be a preoccupation with our selves, with our health, with the need to be in control, or even with worry.

While everyone has a propensity to be and act off-centered, for some people there is a traumatic loss or hurt that has pulled them off center into a false center. Today we are all too aware of the abuse of children that profoundly and agonizingly wounds their souls. It may be emotional or sexual, or physical or verbal abuse. Instead of being affirmed as true and beautiful and good, the child's center of experience is like a deep, black hole. No wonder that those who have been deeply wounded find themselves filling that "hole" with alcohol, food, work, TV, or being busy with many things. All of these things become idols around which life finds its meaning, impoverished as it may be.

In the gospel, Jesus invites Martha, and us, to come home again to the deep place within, that deep place of stillness where we are good and true and beautiful. Thomas Merton speaks of this center as the "true self." The un-centering trauma creates what some call a false self.

Life has a tendency to pull us away from the center. When a person has been deeply wounded, what is experienced is an emptiness, like a dark hole, a bottomless pit.

While such a person continues to relate to God, to self, to others, and to things, the relationships are skewed. Difficult questions arise:

> About God: What kind of God would allow such a thing to happen to a child? How can I trust such a God? I had better take care of myself!
>
> About self: Was I seductive at four years of age? I'm no good; I'm like damaged property. Is everything bad that happens my fault?
>
> About others: Whom can I trust if I cannot trust my parents, grandparents, family, friends, etc.?
>
> About things: I'll prove to the world that I am good. I'll have more degrees, more money, climb the corporate ladder. I'll have more and be better than anyone else. And I'll use things to fill the emptiness. What things? Alcohol, drugs, nicotine, food, work, television, the Internet, etc. For others it may be anxiety or compulsive buying or gambling.

While most of these things are not evil in themselves, and are usually good when used in moderation and when appropriate, they are detrimental to our well-being when the obsession controls us. Power, pleasure, and possessions replace God. St. Ignatius calls them disordered affections; sometimes they become what is called an addiction.

Where there is serious off-centeredness, stemming from childhood abuse, therapy is a great gift to help one discover and begin to heal the early experience. But I believe it is only prayer that brings us home again, back to the center.

All of us, even those who have not been seriously traumatized, have tendencies to be pulled off center. Someone has facetiously suggested that 96 percent of homes are dysfunctional, and no one can find the other 4 percent.

Part of our spiritual journey, part of our "coming home," is to recognize what writer Jean Houston speaks of as "our sacred wound." We carry scars from the hurts we have endured, even if they have only bruised and not broken us. The scars are always there, waiting to trigger what tends to draw us away from living out of the goodness, truth, and beauty that is our true self.

For your consideration and prayerful reflection:

- Where do you find yourself most easily and often off center in your relationship with God, with yourself, with others, or with the use of things?

- About what in your life do you think that Jesus would say to you as to Martha, "you are busy about many things; one thing only is necessary"?

- Are you aware of any unresolved early issues in your life that continue to haunt you, that are in need of healing? With whom can you talk about this and find some help?

- Listen to Jesus as he says to you, "Come to me you who labor and are overburdened, and I will give you rest. Shoulder my yoke and learn from me, for I am gentle and humble in heart and you will find rest for your souls" (Mt 11:28–30).

four

When We Are Uncentered

*For lack of a shepherd they have
scattered, to become the prey of any
wild animal; they have scattered far.
My flock is straying this way and
that, on mountains and high hills;
my flock has been scattered all over
the country. . . .*

—Ezekiel 34:5–6

The word "scattered" is an apt synonym for the experience of being uncentered. Rather than being gathered together in a single-hearted/single-eyed focus, there is a lack of harmony in the life of one who lives out of the dark hole of having been traumatized. This can be true even when the uncenteredness is part of the natural lack of wholeness that seems to be the heritage of us all as human creatures.

For the person who lives uncentered there is an effort to numb the pain and to seek those ways and those things that we imagine will fill the emptiness, and give us some measure of control. The uncentered person looks outside self for salvation and is ruled by "shoulds." This same dynamic is true when uncenteredness is triggered in any of us. Each facet of our lives is colored and shaped by an effort to cope with the uncenteredness.

Not surprisingly, for a person whose early life was disrupted by severe abuse, his or her relationship with God will be filled with fear. Prayer will be less a trustful surrender to a loving Father, and more of a bargaining—trying harder, praying more prayers in an effort to placate and to win the favor of God. A literalism regarding what is expected by God by way of prayer and moral practices will terrorize not only the individual, but those who move in his or her circle of relationships. Confusion and a deep seated anger with God, and/or with the church will cripple the individual.

With relationship to self, the uncentered person lacks a clear sense of self, often succumbing to poor self-esteem, even self-hatred. This is sometimes confused with humility. Anxiety may lead to self-abnegation, to seeing oneself as a victim, given to self-pity. It may show up in a lack of self-care, or on the other hand in being preoccupied with one's appearance.

Gifts will be denied and remain buried. There will be a lack of joy and a lack of leisure and play.

Relationships with others may be co-dependent relationships. There are expectations of others that show up in a critical, demanding, envious attitude that alienates would-be friends.

Finally, the uncentered person is prone to a compulsive use of alcohol, drugs, nicotine, food, or work, in an attempt to fill the emptiness of that uncentered pit that has been hollowed out within him or her. Such things as clothing, exercise, anxiety, sadness, and fear can also be an expression of the uncenteredness when they are compulsively pursued or wallowed in. Needs and wants are confused. Just as the uncentered person can feel that he or she is not enough, there is also a tendency to feel that one never has enough.

While it is painful to come to grips with what it is in our lives that tends to trigger our drift off the center, and what it is that we use to try to fill the emptiness of our false self, it is also a great gift to recognize what the underlying area of dis-ease is in our life, and even, eventually to come to know what spawned it.

A woman I know said that for years she struggled, having a sense that something within her was awry, but not being able to identify it. She was a successful professional woman who was highly praised for her competence and for her generosity in doing for others. Yet the angst continued and pervaded her prayer, her relationships, and in some ways even her work.

During a week of retreat, she begged God to show her what it was that was keeping her from what she sensed she was being called to be and do. Eventually, she came to a sense of what it was that was triggering the unrest. She went to confession—still in the old box confessional—and asked for healing and forgiveness for her "need to be in control." She was actually relieved to have come to the realization that this was an area of darkness, and how it was affecting her prayer, her work beyond the call of duty, and how it blocked true and intimate relationships. So, she confessed it, but suddenly, the priest boomed out in a big voice, "That's no sin; do you have anything else?" Eventually he did give her absolution. Later in the week when she met a longtime friend and told him of what was for her an amazing insight about her need to be in control, he said, "Yes, indeed." It was then, she said, that she experienced the forgiveness. Here was someone who had known this fault in her, but it had not deterred his caring and friendship. And it was, for her, an experience of God.

Only several years later, again in prayer, did she come to realize that the need to be in control was related to the death of her father when she was in her early teens. Without an older brother to lean on, and not wanting to further burden her mother who was in deep grief, she took control of herself and her life. This pattern grew with her and spilled over into all aspects of her life.

She said that now, whenever she is aware of moving into a control mode, she can remind herself that she is no longer thirteen, and the compulsion is modified.

The example reminds us that even if one has not been traumatically abused and de-centered as a child, all of us have had experiences that are wounding. Certain circumstances can pull us out of our center into modes of acting and thinking that are disruptive and counterproductive.

The admission of our woundedness is not a matter for self-denigration, but simply the recognition that we are creatures, that all of us carry within us the frailty as well as the majesty of being human beings created in the image and likeness of God.

In the gospel it is the leper who admits his leprosy, the woman who acknowledges her hemorrhaging, the bent over woman who could not deny her condition, the blind man who cried out for healing, who met and experienced the compassion of Christ. For us, too, it is an incredible grace and gift to know what it is in our lives that keeps us from being centered in Christ, that keeps us from living our lives to the full.

For your consideration and prayerful reflection:

* Reread this chapter. With what phrases or attitudes do you identify? Ask God to show you how they may be hindering you in your journey to wholeness, to God.

- Read the public life of Jesus in one of the gospels. Be attentive to the people that he heals. Choose one of these stories and imagine that you are the person in need of healing. Let yourself meet Jesus in the story; keep your eyes on him; ask him to relieve you of the area of woundedness of which you are aware.

five

Deep Within

*Didn't you realize that you were God's
temple and the Spirit of God was
living among you?*

—1 Corinthians 3:16

It is one thing to speak of our true self as true and good
and beautiful. But there is another truth that is mostly unknown, often not realized. It is almost as if it were a secret.
It is an incredible mystery! It is this: God dwells deep within
each of us, as in a tabernacle, in a sacred place in the depths
of our being.

St. John of the Cross wrote of this reality. He asks the
questions about where God has hidden himself and says that
"the Word, together with the Father and the Holy Spirit, is

hidden essentially in the inmost centre of the soul." He goes on to quote St. Augustine who in speaking to God says, "I found Thee not, O Lord, without, because I erred in seeking Thee without that wert within." John concludes, that God "is, then, hidden within the soul, and there the good contemplative must seek Him...." (*Spiritual Canticle*, Stanza 1, 4)

There is, as the poet Gerard Manley Hopkins says, "the deepest freshness deep down things" and deep down within the human soul, God dwells. God dwells within you as in a tabernacle, only God and you. Always, forever, at this very moment, God is breathing you into life, cherishing you, healing and freeing you, inviting you into incredible intimacy.

It is as if one must turn to poetry to relish this wonderful truth. Simple logic cannot express what is essentially a mystery to be believed. In her poem, "For a Child of God," Jessica Powers, a Carmelite sister in the tradition of John of the Cross, writes:

> The saints and mystics
> had a name
> for that deep
> inwardness of flame,
> the height or depth
> or ground or goal
> Which is God's dwelling
> in the soul.

Not *capax Dei* *
do you say;
nor yet
scintilla animae⁑
nor *synderesis*⁂—
all are fair—
but heaven,
because God is there.

All day and when
you wake at night
think of that place
of living light,
yours and within you
and aglow
where only God
and you can go.

None can assail you
in that place
save your own evil,
routing grace.
Not even angels
see or hear,
nor the dark spirits
prowling near.

But there are days
when watching eyes
could guess that you
hold Paradise.
Sometimes the shining
overflows
and everyone
around you knows.

*capacity for God, ** spark of the soul, *** the innate knowledge of first principles in the moral order

We are invited to come home to that inner chamber, that "place of living light."

Thomas Merton, in reflecting on this reality, says that it is "the return to unity, to the ground, the paradisial inner sacred space where the archetypal [person] dwells in peace and in God. The journey to that space moves through a realm of aridity, dualism, dryness and death. There is need for courage and desire, and above all faith, praise, obedience to the inner voice of the spirit and refusal to give up or to compromise."

In other words, there is a place deep within us where God dwells, a place where no man, no woman, no angel, no demon can penetrate. There it is only God and you.

For your consideration and prayerful reflection:

- What does it mean to you that there is a place within you where only God dwells, a place where no man, no woman, no angel nor demon can penetrate?

- Pray, reflect on, memorize the following poem, "In a Cloud of Angels":

> I walk in a cloud of angels.
> God has a throne in the secret of my soul.
> I move, encircled by light,
> blinded by glowing faces,
> lost and bewildered in the motion of wings,
> stricken by music too sublime to bear.
> Splendor is everywhere.

God is always enthroned on the cherubim,
circled by seraphim.
Holy, holy, holy,
wave upon wave of endless adoration.
I walk in a cloud of angels that
worship Him.

—Jessica Powers

s i x

The *Point Vierge*

*And you too, in him, are being built
into a house where God lives, in the
Spirit.*

—Ephesians 2:22

One time at the end of a presentation of this wondrous teaching of the indwelling of God in the center of our souls, one of the women broke the silence to ask a question. Over a number of years she had shared with me her very painful story of sexual abuse, and this in the context of a seriously dysfunctional family. With courage and simplicity, she spoke her question: "Does that mean that I am still virginal in some part of me?" The silence among the women at the gathering of AA and Al-Anon women really deepened. I simply nodded my head, yes. And another woman who had clearly been through much pain and had been in sobriety for a number of years put a fist in the air, and pronounced, "And I choose to believe it."

Thomas Merton has something to say about this profound, virginal place within us. The quotation is long, but well worth reading and pondering.

> I have the immense joy of being [human], a member of a race in which God became incarnate. As if the sorrows and stupidities of the human condition could overwhelm me, now I realize what we all are. And if only everybody could realize this! But it cannot be explained. There is no way of telling people that they are all walking around shining like the sun. . . .
>
> It was as if I suddenly saw the secret beauty of their hearts, the depths of their hearts where neither sin nor desire nor self-knowledge can reach the core of their reality, the person that each one is in God's eyes. If only they could all see themselves as they really are. If only we could see each other that way all the time. There would be no more war, no more hatred, no more cruelty, no more greed. . . .
>
> I suppose that the big problem would be that we would fall down and worship each other. But this cannot be seen, only believed and understood by a particular gift.

Again, that expression, *le point vierge* (I cannot translate it) comes in here. At the center of our being is a point of nothingness which is untouched by sin and by illusion, a point of pure truth, a point or spark which belongs entirely to God, which is never at our disposal, from which God disposes of our lives, which is inaccessible to the fantasies of our own mind or the brutalities of our own will. This little point of nothingness and of absolute poverty is the pure glory of God in us. It is so to speak His name written in us, as our poverty, as our indigence, as our dependence, as our son[/daughter]ship. It is in everybody, and if we could see it we could see these billions of particles of light coming together in the face and blaze of a sun that would make all the darkness and cruelty of life vanish completely. . . . I have no program for this seeing. It is only given. But the gate of heaven is everywhere.

Do you not know that you are the temple of God and that God dwells within you?

For your consideration and prayerful reflection:

- Reread the text and underline those words that particularly strike you. Let them resonate within you. What are the thoughts, the feelings that arise within you?

- Read and reflect (and memorize?) the following passages:

Didn't you realize that you were God's temple
and that the Spirit of God was living among you?
(1 Cor 3:16)

We are only the earthenware jars that hold
this treasure, to make it clear that such an
overwhelming power comes from God and not
from ourselves. (2 Cor 4:7)

If only you knew what God is offering to you. . . .
(Jn 4:10)

seven

Coming Home
to the Center

"Come," my heart says, "Seek his face."
Your face, Lord, do I seek.

—Psalm 27:8 (NRSV)

When we find ourselves seriously off-center in an on-going way, therapy or counseling can be of great help in discovering the sources of our broken spirits. That source may be something as devastatingly painful as a hidden childhood trauma, or it may be part of the give and take, gain and loss that is a normal part of growing up. When therapy can help in understanding the root of our problems, it is a great gift.

But only prayer can help us return to that place deep within us, that place where God dwells, that place where no man or woman, no demon or angel can penetrate.

It is prayer, in a movement in faith, that helps us focus on that inner place where God is even now renewing and healing us. Centering prayer is a contemplative approach to prayer through stillness and focus.

There are moments in each of our lives when we are brought quietly into stillness, for example, peering down into a pool of water, looking up into a starry sky, walking into a dewy morning sunrise over a lake, holding a sleeping child, gazing at a masterpiece, listening to a symphony, being held in a warm embrace.

These are moments we remember and cherish and revisit again and again when our souls are anxious and in need of peace. These memories are the touchstones that lead us into the wordless mystery before which we can only be still.

The psalmist tells us, "Be still and know that I am God" (Ps 46:10, NRSV). In this stillness we meet the mystery of God. When we are still, we cast our trust on God, and in that stillness God's healing power ministers to us. That stillness is an essential part of what we call contemplation.

Through spiritual masters like Thomas Merton, Thomas Keating, and Basil Pennington, contemplative prayer—being still in the presence of God—is once again being made available for everyone. They recommend that each day we spend two twenty-minute periods in this kind of prayer.

While there are times of spontaneous centering, we can intentionally practice this prayer to facilitate the centering in that union and communion with God that is our baptismal call.

The approach is simple:

First find a quiet time and place where there will be minimal disturbance. Relax in body and in spirit. Deep breathing can facilitate this relaxation. Direct your attention and intention to God with a heartfelt prayer such as, "Dear God, I want to be with you in faith and in love."

Then, let yourself sink into the deep place in your soul where God is breathing you into life, that deep place where God holds and cherishes you, and is at this very moment continuing to create and invite and heal you. Rest there.

This exercise prepares the soul to receive the healing ministry of the Holy Spirit, the divine touches of our God.

When and if you become aware of any thoughts and feelings, simply bring yourself back to the center, using a word or phrase like "Jesus," "Abba," "shalom," or "let go." Or choose a word of your own. The use of the word is like a feather, gently bringing your awareness back to that wordless place where God dwells within you.

Close the twenty-minute prayer time by slowly praying the Our Father.

Thomas Keating suggests one such period daily for "maintenance," two for "healing."

To discover whether this approach to prayer is a form suited and helpful to you at this time in your life, make a commitment for a month to praying twice a day, using the process described above.

Like any commitment to prayer, centering prayer is a discipline. Sometimes a person may feel very distracted and need to say the prayer word many times in any one period. On other occasions, the time will pass quickly. One never evaluates the worth or goodness of a prayer period, whether or not it is distracted, etc. William Barry says that it is enough that we simply show up for prayer. "It is enough for me" says the psalmist "to keep my soul still and quiet like a child in its mother's arms" (Ps 131:2).

People who practice this form of prayer on a regular, daily basis discover that their thinking is more clear and decisive, and that they are more peaceful as they go about their day.

When practiced faithfully, centering prayer can begin to heal uncenteredness. One begins to relate to God, to self, to others, and to things in a way that is more serene, clear, peaceful, and free.

For your consideration and prayerful reflection:

- Reread and make your own this method of centering prayer; commit yourself to the practice of this approach over the coming month.

eight

The Door Is Everywhere

*"Look, I am standing at the door,
knocking. If one of you hears me
calling and opens the door, I will come
in to share his meal."*

—Revelation 3:20

While centering prayer is clearly a classic and extremely helpful way for maintaining a focused life, there are other ways that complement the use of centering prayer on a regular basis.

Keating and Pennington, in promoting centering prayer, make clear that it is essential to stay in touch and grounded in the Word of God. In true Benedictine tradition they encourage the use of an approach to praying with scripture called *lectio divina*, freely translated as Sacred Reading.

Lectio divina is a "full-person" approach to praying with scripture. In includes reading a passage, a meditative reflection on that passage, and then a spontaneous prayer that flows from the content of one's reading and reflection. Ideally, it closes with a contemplative centering on what has moved the person in prayer during this process.

Whenever one picks up the scripture for prayer, the word that touches us is truly a door through which we pass into the presence of our God, dwelling within and speaking to our hearts.

The rosary, a favorite approach to prayer for generations of Catholics, offers mantra-like repetition that draws one into an interior quiet and stillness in the presence of our God.

One cannot speak of the various means to centering without mentioning the sacramental moments of eucharist, reconciliation, and healing that are integral to our experience of church community.

And beyond spoken or written words and even sacred actions, there are things and events that also "speak" to our hearts and therefore can be a way of drawing us to the center of our lives. As theologian Richard McBrien says:

> Everything is, in principle, capable of embodying and communicating the divine. There is no finite instrument that God cannot put to use. On the other hand, we humans have nothing else apart

> from finite instruments to express our own
> response to God's self-communication. Just as
> the divine reaches us through the finite, so we
> reach the divine through the finite.

The word of God has, in the Judeo-Christian tradition, held a primacy. But early on the word included not only the spoken (or written) word, but actions and things that "spoke." So, for the Jewish people, deliverance by God from the oppression of Egypt was a mighty and strong "word" that spoke to them about the identity of their God. And all of creation, the fruit of God's creating word, spoke of God's beauty, majesty, mystery.

So too for us. A magnificent sunset, the soft stirring breeze across the lake on a hot summer day, the sun dogs that shimmer on either side of an afternoon sun in subzero weather, the appearance of a small flower in the cracks of the pavement of a busy city street speak to us. These "things" speak to us of a mystery, of God. They draw us into a moment, a center of awareness and of peace, of thanksgiving and praise. Subtly, incredibly, such moments shape our inward hearts.

Gifts can be a reminder and a call to the center, sometimes almost unconsciously. For example, years ago I was given a delicate, hand-crafted doily. It probably came from France in the early part of the twentieth century when our Sisters first came to establish a school in northwestern Minnesota. It is LePuy lace, made in the city where our congregation was founded in 1650. It is the kind of lace that has for centuries been made by the women of that city. In the seventeenth century, women often gathered in circles to make their lace while listening to someone who could read, or while praying the rosary together. Though the doily is frayed in spots, its presence on my coffee table is a precious connection to those first women who were Sisters of St. Joseph and to the gift of their lives.

On the center of that doily, I have placed a statue of Mary, also from France, also a gift. The statue is only about eight inches tall, terra cotta in color. Mary is slightly bent, holding the Child, but in a gesture of offering him to the world. From one position she seems incredibly young; from the back she seems eternally old and bent.

I light a candle before her when I pray in the early morning; during December she is the centerpiece of my Advent wreath. In a wordless way, the doily and the Mary statue are "words" that speak to my soul. It is enough to sit in their presence and to center myself within.

No doubt, even the description of the doily, statue, and candle indirectly describes my own deeper hope and dream, and perhaps also, God's deeper desire for me.

There was a time when a crucifix hung in a prominent place in each home, sometimes in each room of a Catholic home. It drew one's eyes, often was the focus for family prayer.

One of the things we love about coming home is being in the presence, not only of the people who best know and love us, but of those things that hold memories, that reconnect us to who and what we are. And that is what we miss when we no longer have a home to which we can return.

For your consideration and prayerful reflection:

- What are some passages of scripture that have, in your own life, given you focus?

- What are the approaches to prayer that are most congenial, most helpful in drawing you to the center?

- What are the memories that bring you back to who you really are in the centermost part of your being?

- What things do you treasure as "doorways" to the sacred? Describe one of them. What do your words say about your own spiritual life, your dreams, your hopes?

nine

Center to Center

"Love one another, just as I have loved you."

—John 13:34

How does God love us? We believe, on the word and example of Jesus, that God looks on us with infinite, unconditional compassion, that when God looks at us he sees the depths of who we are, sees and embraces the center of our being. It is a forgiving, tenderly kind, and faithful love.

So what does it mean for us to love one another?

Let us consider that if it is true that each of us has that center wherein God dwells, so then does every other person we meet.

Every other person has this center; each person invites our reverence. As Thomas Merton says, if only we could, all the time, see ourselves the way we really are, "there would be no more war, no more hatred, no more cruelty, no more greed. . . ." We cannot grow in our own contemplative centeredness without all of our relating being affected.

Most of the time for most of us, the reality of the indwelling of God in ourselves as well as in others is a matter of faith. But occasionally we do seem to catch a glimpse of another's center. Something clicks; we know; we see! And when the experience is mutual, it is nothing short of amazing.

When two people really fall in love, it is because they catch a glimpse of each other's center. It happens, of course, between a man and a woman—and it is more than a matter of sexual attraction. It happens in friendship between men or women, or even between a teacher and a student, or a doctor and a patient, or a counselor and a counselee. There is a recognition of each other's center. It is mysterious; one cannot make it happen; it is hard to explain, but when it is there, we know.

Often when a young man and a young woman are in love and contemplating marriage, a parent will say, sometimes in exasperation, sometimes with loving amusement, "I don't know what he sees in her," or "I don't know what she sees in him." But if it is to be an enduring relationship, this mutual awareness is the foundation.

This connection to each other's center can be difficult to maintain. It can easily happen that we relate in an off-centered way.

Let us take the example of a young couple, Mary and Joe, who have been married for three or four months. They love each other, were attracted initially by that mutual awareness of the deep center of each other, although they probably would not speak of it in that way. They gave themselves time to foster that friendship.

It is getting near five o'clock and Mary is at home. She came home early this day because she had a bad headache, part of premenstrual stress. And since she was home early, she decided to make a nice supper for Joe. However, her headache distracted her and she has burned the casserole.

Let me tell you a bit about her background. She grew up in what one would call a dysfunctional family, the eldest daughter to a father who was an alcoholic and regularly drank up his paycheck. When he was drinking, he had a tendency to be inappropriate in fondling his wife in the presence of the children, much to their disgust. Mary grew up determined never to marry an alcoholic, and that she would never live in scarcity. She found in Joe a man who is loving and attentive. So, as five o'clock draws near, we find her with a headache, and disappointed about the burned supper.

Meanwhile, as five o'clock draws near, Joe is summoned to the office of his boss. Joe grew up in a basically good home. His mother frequently, or so it seemed to him, would tell him that she didn't know how he would ever be able to support a family. While she would say she was only teasing, those words have branded his soul, so that he struggles with self-doubt. As for alcohol, he can take or leave it. It is one of the things that Mary appreciates about him. But now as he walks to the office, he is attacked by the self-doubt. He is among the last to have been hired; what if he is being let go?

When Joe enters the office, his supervisor comes around the desk and shakes his hand and says, "Joe, I just want to congratulate you on the fine way you handled that recent job. Here is a bonus and you are right in line for a promotion." Joe's first thought is of Mary, and how he can't wait to tell her the good news. But his supervisor says, "Let's celebrate with a drink." He pulls out a bottle of liquor from his desk drawer, and each has a small glass.

Joe can hardly wait to get home to see Mary. As he opens the door to their home, he joyfully shouts, "Mary, where are you?" and as she walks into the room, he throws his arms around her and kisses her.

You can guess what happens. She smells the alcohol on his breath; she is transported back to her childhood home when her father came home drunk, and threw his arms around her mother. And given the vulnerability of the pain of her headache and the disappointment about the supper, she may suddenly find herself pulling away and screeching at Joe. "Have you been drinking? I told you I would never marry an alcoholic." The experience has triggered an off-centeredness in Mary, so that she is pulled into the experience of her childhood pain.

If Joe is snagged by his own self-doubt, he will find himself getting angry, and shouting at her, "No wonder your father drank, if that is the way your mother yelled at him" and so on. And the conversation, or shouting match, will be from off-center to off-center, and things will be said that will take a long time to heal.

But, if Joe can maintain his own sense of center, and keep focused on this woman that he loves and cares for, if he can speak from his own center, not to the "hurt little girl" in her, but to her center, he may find himself saying, "Mary, what's wrong? Did you have a hard day?" And she may begin to cry. He can possibly say, "Let me get you some tea and then let me hear about it."

She may well say at this point, "I don't know why I yelled at you like that; I know that you don't drink. I just get so afraid. I've had a headache all day and then I burned the supper."

And he can say, "Hey, I've got some good news to share with you, and let's go out for supper to a really nice place, because part of the good news is that we can afford it."

This is an example that is repeated in many of our relational circumstances—with a co-worker, or with a neighbor, or with a family member.

Note that Joe cannot "bring" Mary back to her center, but by speaking from his center to her center, she can find her own way back there.

Another's off-centeredness can pull us off-center. So it is important to find ways, sometimes with a temporary distancing, to be able to resume a conversation that is centered.

When one is aware that someone else seems to be coming not from his or her best self, it is always possible, though not always easy, to respond not from our own off-centeredness but from our center to the center of the other.

Another story that comes to mind is one that a friend told me about her and her husband's experience. After being married about three years, "Joan" and "Jim" found themselves almost constantly at odds with each other. The concern was deep enough that they decided to seek counseling. The counselor met with the two of them together. The counselor said to Jim, "Why did you marry Joan?" and Jim began to recount all the qualities in Joan that had first attracted him, and all the things he loved about her. Of course Joan was hearing all the positive and complimentary things he said about her. The counselor said to him, "Are these qualities and things still true of Joan?" "Indeed, yes," Jim said.

Then she turned and asked Joan the same question, and Joan listed all the things, all the qualities in Jim, that had initially attracted her to him, and of course, Jim was hearing her. And when asked, she responded, "Yes, he still has all those qualities."

Joan told me that at that point in the visit to the counselor, she and Jim looked at each other, smiled, took each other by the hand, and left the counseling office. They had rediscovered the gifts of the inner center that had first drawn them together.

In a relationship, each person is committed to keeping that center-to-center relationship alive. Anniversaries, when stories of beginnings of the relationship are shared, are often an occasion of renewing that center-to-center awareness. Oftentimes recommitments are made by the renewal of vows.

Of course, this kind of relating, from one's own center to the center of the other, is not limited to those who are close to us, but in faith we can bring this kind of perspective to everyone we meet, even casually.

Several years ago, a young woman named Ashley Smith came to national attention when she was able to persuade a suspected killer who was being hunted by police for a shooting spree in Atlanta, not to kill her. She reported that she had talked to him about God's power, told him to fulfill his destiny by surrendering to the police and finding a way, in prison, to fulfill his destiny by sharing the word of God with other inmates. Although she would not have spoken of it this way, she was able to stay centered herself, and to believe in and relate to the center of a man who was threatening to kill her.

For your consideration and prayerful reflection:

- Think of someone with whom you have experienced a center-to-center experience of relationship. What are the qualities that describe your relationship? How does that relationship support you in the hard times?

- Think of someone with whom your relationship seems uncentered, someone whose words or actions seem to trigger your own off-centeredness. What's one thing you can do to bring it to a center-to-center relationship?

- As you watch TV or read the newspaper, be aware, from the perspective of center-to-center relations, of stories of broken relationships, but also of heroism.

- Reflect on these words of St. Paul:

  > "Do not let your love be a pretence, but sincerely prefer good to evil. Love each other as much as brothers [and sisters] should, and have a profound respect for each other. . . . If any of the saints are in need you must share with them; and you should make hospitality your special care." (Rom 12:9–10, 11)

ten

Supporting Center-to-Center Relationships

> *Finally, all of you, have unity of*
> *spirit, sympathy, love for one another,*
> *a tender heart, and a humble mind.*
> *Do not repay evil for evil or abuse for*
> *abuse; but on the contrary, repay with*
> *a blessing.*

—1 Peter 3:8–9 (NRSV)

Ilia Delio reminds us that in all our relationships we are called "to look beneath the surface of the fragile flesh of the other into the depths of the reality before us. We cannot see clearly outwardly, unless we can see clearly inwardly."

There is an approach to prayer that can support our efforts to enter into and to sustain center-to-center relationships.

In their book, *Kything: The Art of Spiritual Presence*, Louis Savary and Patricia Berne have written about this kind of prayer. According to the dictionary, to kythe (rhymes with tithe) means "to make known or to become known." To kythe is to make your true self present to another. It is a spiritual presence and meeting of the core, or heart, of one person with the core of another. It is a prayer of union and spiritual presence.

While the word "kything" may be unfamiliar to us, the experience is quite common. Have you ever thought of someone you love and in your remembering and imaging the person, felt as if you were in his or her presence? Have you experienced what could only be called an exchange of love and peace and energy? You may have felt strengthened and renewed in the gift offer, and your faith told you that your loved one was somehow also strengthened and supported.

Parents often experience this when their children are away at school. Lovers and friends know this kind of communication over distances. It is a kind of indwelling. And when that exchange is a conscious sending of the love and peace of God, it a consoling and wonderful kind of prayer.

Savary and Berne find a biblical basis for kything in the words of Jesus: "If anyone loves me, they will keep my word, and my Father will love him[/her], and we shall come and make our home within him[/her]" (Jn 14:23).

While it is possible to kythe with Christ or a saint, it is especially helpful in supporting those relationships that we want to be an authentic center-to-center experience.

There are four steps to this approach to prayer:

First, center within your own heart, in your own truest self. Once in touch with your inner self, ask God to gift you and your kything partner with the Holy Spirit.

Second, when you are ready, image the person with whom you want to kythe. Be aware of his or her center. Image the love in your heart, like light, flowing from your heart to the heart of your kything partner, penetrating and enfolding that person in the warmth of your care, in the love that God has placed within you for that person.

Third, open yourself to receive the love and energy that flows to you from your kything partner. Welcome the gift, and rest in the mutual exchange of love and energy. It is like light flowing from you to the other and from the other to you.

Close your prayer by thanking God for the gifts that have come to you through the other person. Ask God to bless your kything partner.

Kything makes possible a deeper kind of presence between people, for it invites not only a physical and psychological presence, but a spiritual presence.

Kything can be done across the breakfast table, or it can be done over distances, sending the energy of Christ's and our own love and peace across the miles. It can happen during a conversation, even a painful one, without the other person even being aware of it. It is a tender way of communicating with those who are sick and not able to respond; it is a powerful form of communication when mutually agreed upon between two people who care about each other.

For your consideration and prayerful reflection:

- Consider a person with whom you have a deep and loving relationship. Using the four steps above, spend some time kything with that person.

eleven

Living in an Uncentered World

> *"I am going to take you from among
> the nations and gather you from all
> the foreign countries, and bring you
> home to your own land."*
>
> **—Ezekiel 36:24**

We know that it is not only individuals that can be uncentered and out of focus. Daily we are impacted by the world around us. We live and try to be faithful in churches that have been fractured by scandals. We endeavor to make sense of living in a nation, terrorized by fear, and confused by government leaders who seem intent on war in the name of some eventual peace. Our children cannot walk to school alone in safety, or be assured of security within the classroom—or sadly, even within their homes. There is no family that has not been affected by divorce. Our entertainment offers a menu of violence. At every turn we are urged toward a consumerism that promises fulfillment with a slimmer body, or a bigger car, or a larger house in a more prestigious part of the city, and on and on.

We live in a broken world. Something is clearly out of focus.

And it is not new! And it is not easy.

In the history of Israel, we see how the people of God struggled to stay in harmony with God's promise and plan for them, with their center.

For the Jewish people, the center of their country was Jerusalem, the holy city, and within the city was the center of worship, the temple. And in the temple, in the innermost sanctuary, was the holy of holies where God dwelt. Each year, in spirit if not in body, the people gathered in the temple to experience themselves as a people of the covenant.

Rooted in the deepest and most original story of the Jewish people was the mystery of God's love for them. "You will be my people and I will be your God." It was to God they turned in time of trouble; it was to God that they looked for guidance. Unlike other nations whose king was considered a god, for Israel, the human king merely stood in for God who was king, and shepherd and Lord of the people. Faithfulness to the covenant assured security.

As such, alliances with foreign nations were forbidden. However, eventually the leadership succumbed to the pressures of those nations that were attempting to gain control over Israel and Judea because this narrow country between the Mediterranean Sea and the desert was a key trade route between Egypt and the Mesopotamian kingdoms.

Alliances were made, contrary to the understanding of the covenant. Part of each alliance was to send a royal daughter to the other king. Thus the women in harem of the king in Jerusalem each represented a foreign alliance. In addition, these women were allowed to bring their gods; in the shadow of the temple, shrines to these other gods were tolerated.

Gradually the national spirit was weakened. Waves of armies from the north, the Assyrians, and later the Babylonians, and then the Persians swept down toward Jerusalem. Eventually Jerusalem succumbed to the enemy.

The leaders and all the people of influence and their families were forcibly gathered together in the center of the city, and with the few possessions they could carry they were marched off to Babylon, a trek of a thousand miles.

Contrary to what had happened to the people of the northern kingdom when they were conquered and exiled to other countries where they became part of the new culture and lost their own identity, the people who went to Babylon were able to maintain their own sense of community and identity. They met weekly with their priest and prophet who went into exile with them, and brought with him the sacred scrolls with the story of the covenant, of God's intervention with Abraham, and the story of the Exodus. It was during this time that the scriptures became "a home away from home."

They would have had news from the homeland, of the death of the king, of the collapse of their nation, of the destruction of their beautiful temple. And they would have known that as leaders and people of influence they had had a part in that failure. They had not warned, nor stood up against the king and his cronies as he had acted contrary to the covenant. They grieved the loss of their center.

> Beside the streams of Babylon we sat and wept
> at the memory of Zion,
> leaving our harps hanging on the poplars there....
> How could we sing one of Yahweh's hymns
> in a pagan country?
> Jerusalem, if I forget you, may my right hand
> wither! (Ps 137:1, 4–5)

The people learned a lot in exile. They came to a new appreciation for what they thought they had lost; they experienced their lives in a new way, seeing themselves in exile like the children of Israel who lived in oppression in Egypt. They found God, not in the temple, but in the midst of their community, and learned that God was not only their God, but a God that transcended geography and embraced all people as his own. And they began to turn their hearts to God, trusting, hoping again in the promise.

And then, through Ezekiel, God spoke to them, reassuring them regarding the Promised Land. He said to them,

> "I am going to take you from among the nations and gather you together from all the foreign countries, and bring you home to your own land. I shall pour clean water over you and you will be cleansed; I shall cleanse you of all your defilement and all your idols. I shall give you a new heart, and put a new spirit in you. . . . You will live in the land which I gave your ancestors. You shall be my people and I will be your God."
> (Ez 36:24–26, 28)

The exile was real, as were the loss and painful separations that accompanied it. But somehow, in the bigger story of their people and God's faithfulness, they found hope and renewal of life. They found their way back to the center.

For your consideration and prayerful reflection:

- In what ways do you personally experience the world, the institutions that make it up, as broken and unfocused?

- Where in our world are you aware of those people or movements who are pondering the situation in the greater story as is found in the scripture?

- Prayerfully reread Ezekiel 36:16–38. Highlight what especially touches you. Let those words resonate deeply within your own heart.

- Pray Psalm 137.

twelve

Living Centered in an Uncentered World

Here is my servant whom I uphold,
my chosen one in whom my soul
delights.
I have endowed him with my spirit
that he may bring true justice to the
nations.

—Isaiah 42:1

It is one thing to read about a nation, such as that of the Jewish people from the sixth century BC who, unfaithful to the covenant, found themselves in exile, having truly lost their center, and who gradually, through the strength of Ezekiel, their priest and prophet and through historical circumstances, returned to their homeland. From hindsight it all seems predictable and even inevitable.

It is another thing altogether to find oneself in situations where the structures upon which we have depended seem to be crumbling. How do we stay centered in an uncentered world? How do we act in such a way as to neither "waver, nor be crushed?" (Is 42:3).

Workers on the precipice of retiring with a pension from a factory in which they have loyally contributed their working hours for thirty or more years find themselves let go short of the years needed for retirement benefits. The factory that was founded to render a needed service to society is focused not on the service, but on the bottom line.

A parish council meets to respond to the needs of the parishioners as they have made them known through a questionnaire. The plurality of people say that they are concerned about the teenagers and would like to see the religious education program strengthened with the hiring of a youth minister. The pastor says that there is no money for this project, since he has decided to put in new carpeting throughout the church.

A couple continue to put off having a family because they are building a bank account and want first of all to have a bigger house, a new car, and upscale travel and vacations before beginning a family.

A religious order succumbs to the concern for retirement planning and the bulk of resources are invested in retirement, with little to encourage and support new and needed ministries.

A diocese refuses to allow lay men or women to administer priestless parishes, imposing greater burdens on those priests who continue to be faithful and obedient in spite of aging.

These are a few examples of people or institutions that have lost their center or at least have moved into an off centeredness. As any institution or organization loses its central focus, people become disillusioned and it eventually dies.

> Where there is no vision, the people perish.
> (Pr 29:18)

It is not that every institution is in this situation, but we know that a life-giving and vibrant institution needs to make a continual effort to renew its central purpose.

An institution or organization that is centered will clearly have a needed service as its purpose. It will be people-centered and foster growth and wholeness not only to the people served, but for the people who are part of giving that service. It is characterized by a circle of care in which the structure serves the people. It is future-oriented.

An uncentered institution has as its purpose the accumulation of money. People are dispensable, and are used to serve that purpose. Rather than people-centered, it is commodity-centered. Hierarchical in approach, people must serve the structure, and so are bound by the way things have always been.

In necessarily being a part of an institution, often a number of them simultaneously, it is helpful to keep in mind that an instruction or any organization or process is simply a container for transformation. It is never an end in itself. It is meant to maximize the development and use of the gifts of the people who are part of it, and to foster a fullness of life, creativity, and well-being. It is a matter of justice that people are supported not only by a financial recompense but by being provided by an environment that is healing and freeing.

The administrative head and his/her management assistants are servants of the central purpose of the organization.

So, how does one remain personally centered in an uncentered situation, or how does one contribute to the health of an institution?

First of all, it is important that the individual maintain a personal balance and centeredness through reflection and prayer.

Second, the individual in whatever capacity he or she serves in the institution can continue to maintain and help focus on the central purpose. As issues arise, it may mean asking how a particular action will carry out the stated purpose of the institution. Many organizations spend much time and even money defining a mission statement, which is then relegated to a drawer and never mentioned until the next annual review.

Third, it means acting and speaking with compassion, even in difficult situations. Administration and leadership is not an easy task, and is made more difficult in our times because of the constant change that is a part of our world. It calls for continually creating what was once believed to be static. Approaching an administrator, pastor, or a spouse with compassion means being open to hear her or his rationale before proceeding in coming to a decision.

Finally, it is helpful to keep a sense of perspective, balance, and humor. Twenty years from now how will I remember this situation? How do I want to remember it? God is bigger than our biggest problems.

For your consideration and prayerful reflection:

- Name an institution that you have experienced as centered. What was your experience of being part of such a situation? How did it contribute to a fullness of life for all concerned?

- Name an institution that you experience as uncentered. What one thing can you do to help move that institution toward centeredness?

- In those institutions in which you are a member, what keeps you faithful? What does faithfulness mean today?

- Prayerfully reflect on the First Song of the Servant of Yahweh, Isaiah 42:1–4. How are you inspired by these words in your own endeavor to bring true justice to your world?

---
thirteen

To the God of Jesus

> *"Come to me all you who labor and are overwhelmed and I will give you rest. Shoulder my yoke and learn from me, for I am gentle and humble in heart and you will find rest for your souls."*

—Matthew 11:28–29

Who is this God who dwells in the center of our souls? What is this God like? How does this God look upon the creatures of his hand?

If we have grown up with a God who is like a policeman who is always on the lookout for our misdemeanors, or if the

God we know is like a judge who metes out punishment, or like an angry parent, then it will not be surprising that we resist meeting this God within or without ourselves.

As Christians we look to Jesus to "show us the Father" (Jn 14:8). If we want to know what God is like, we contemplate Jesus who is the Word of God spoken in time, the "translation" of all that God is into human terms.

In the gospel, we watch Jesus as he moves across the dusty roads from Nazareth to Jerusalem, from the Sea of Galilee to Cana. We see him inviting people to be part of his life; we see him reaching out to touch and heal lepers. We watch as he gathers his disciples around him to question them, to teach them. We see people attracted to him, and when they are hungry he finds the means to feed them. He is gentle; he is strong. He is kind and compassionate, even stepping beyond his own perceived timing to respond to his mother's concern for the embarrassment of a newly married couple. He never sidesteps his deep integrity, but responds directly to the Pharisees when they challenge him and his way. We see him embracing little children; we see him tired at the end of the day and thirsty; we watch as he draws away into the night to pray.

Jesus is affirming and compassionate; he is forgiving and freeing; he is creative and challenging, and he gives hope to the hopeless.

By contemplating Jesus in action, we come to know our God as affirming and compassionate, as forgiving and freeing, as creative and challenging, and as the source of our hope and integrity.

We see Jesus in action and each action witnesses to the God who is the center of his heart and being. We listen to his words. He often told stories drawing on the experiences of the people who listened.

Luke 15 contains three stories that Jesus told. The stories are about a lost sheep, a lost coin, and a lost son—or actually, two lost sons.

While these stories are frequently used to catechize parishioners about their own "lostness," Jesus' focus is less on the lost than on the God who goes out looking and finds us.

In the first story, Jesus tells of a shepherd who had a hundred sheep. One wandered off and was lost. And Jesus tells us that the shepherd leaves the ninety-nine to go looking for the one lost sheep. Perhaps it got snagged in some thorn bushes, so that the more it tried to get freed, the more entangled and stuck it got. Jesus' story invites us to see the shepherd searching and then finding the lost sheep. We can picture the shepherd, with tender fingers, gradually dislodging the sheep from its trap. And then, because no doubt the sheep was exhausted and possibly injured, the shepherd lifts the sheep, smelly as it would have been, and places it on his shoulders to carry it home again. And if that were not enough, when he returns to the fold, the shepherd says to the other shepherds, "Rejoice with me, for that which was lost has been found!"

What an image of God—concerned, searching, going to the place where the sheep is most lost and entangled, risking the pain of the thorns, gently carrying that weak creature. Like Jesus himself, the shepherd is compassionate and caring, healing and forgiving, and deeply happy to bring home the one who is lost.

Surely the story of the lost sheep would have resonated with the people who listened to Jesus, for sheep and shepherds were a part of their daily experience.

But in the event that they had not caught the message about this God that Jesus came to witness, he told another story.

This story was about a woman who lost a coin and cleaned her whole house in an effort to find it. No doubt among the poor the loss of a coin was significant. But scripture scholars tell us that this coin was probably one of ten that a woman received from her husband-to-be. She would have worn with pride these coins strung on a light cord or chain on her forehead. What Jesus does not say, but the people who listened would also have known, was that if a husband had reason to *think* that his wife was unfaithful, he could jerk off one of the coins. No wonder, then, that this good woman panics and cleans the whole house in search of the coin, which she eventually does find. And with relief, calls in her friends to rejoice with her.

Again, Jesus is telling us that God is like this woman who, when something or someone is lost, will go into the dusty corners seeking the one who is lost, and again, is filled with joy at the finding. The parable is especially telling in that we, like the coin, are a part of the covenant that God has with each of us. We are precious to God.

And in the event that we still have not caught the realization of how compassionate and loving our God is, Jesus tells a story that touches each of those men and women who listened, for they all knew what it meant to be part of a family, either in their experience of being children, or being parents themselves.

The story that Jesus tells is of a father who has two sons, the youngest of whom asks for his inheritance and takes off for unknown places. No doubt the father's heart was wounded as that child, the younger of the two, left whistling a merry tune with his belongings in his knapsack and his father's money in his pocket. While we hear what happens to this son as he squanders the money and finally pawns his belongings, even his ring, our concern and awareness is on the father, who knows that his son is in trouble, who grieves for what may be happening to him, whose own heart is lonely for the sound of the voice of this loved child. We have to believe it was not happenstance that the father finally sees the bedraggled young man limping back home down the road, but that there was not an hour when the father did not think of him, there was not an evening when he did not sit on the porch with his eyes focused on the road even as the night darkened. And when the son finally appears, the father races down the steps, and down the road toward the young man, not waiting for him. And he throws his arms around the young man, smelly and ragged as he is, and brings him home. He feeds him, has him bathed and his wounds tended to, and gives him new clothing, a ring that reinstates him as a son, and shoes for his feet—for only free men wore shoes.

In his story, Jesus also tells us about the "other" son, not only about the son who squandered all of the father's gifts, but the one who stayed home, who is self-righteous. He always did the right thing, but for the wrong reason. And here, too, we see the father going out to the son, not waiting for him to come in to him, and when the son explodes with anger and resentment, saying that he has "slaved" for his father, the father gently but firmly reasons with him, and reassures him that all he has is his, but that it is right to rejoice in the lost son who has returned.

Jesus says this is what our God is like! Everything you say about the father, you can say about the God of Jesus and our God.

The God that Jesus reveals through his actions and through his words is a God who cares and draws near, a God whose compassion has no bounds and who comes seeking us in the places where we are most lost.

Truly, this is the God whom Ilia Delio calls "unstoppable goodness—a God who simply can't wait to give everything away and to love us where we are" (Delio, p. 31).

And this is the God who has found a home deep within the human heart of each of us.

For your consideration and prayerful reflection:

- Read chapter 15 in Luke in its entirety. Which story most touches your heart?

- Who was God for you as a child? How did you imagine God? Was the way you learned about God frightening or consoling and loving?

- What are the experiences in your life that have helped you understand God in an ever more loving and creative way?

- Read through one of the gospels and simply watch Jesus as he interacts with the people in his life, with his disciples, with the poor and sick, with his enemies. What does his life show you about the mystery of God?

fourteen

The Journey

"If the road is too long for you, if . . .
the place in which Yahweh chooses to
make a home for his name is too far,
when Yahweh your God has blessed
you . . . you must go to the place chosen
by Yahweh. . . ."

—Deuteronomy 14:24–25

To come home to that deep place within us, to come to know the God of our lives, to arrive at that integrated wholeness that is God's dream for each of us is a journey. It has a beginning in a moment of conversion and call, and it has an end point of arrival, perhaps only totally realized in the embrace of God that will be our death.

Between that beginning and end point, we travel on foot, sometimes barefoot over gravel and hot sand. Sometimes we may be carried on wings. And sometimes we may realize that we have abandoned the journey and set up housekeeping by the side of the road. There will be times when the inner urgings of our hearts will stir up the Spirit within us and prompt us to stand up, and to set off again in search for our true home.

The journey is often long and searching. In the words of one writer, there is the suggestion that "if instead of using the expression 'spiritual life,' we used 'the seeking,' we should set out from the beginning and go on to the end with a clearer idea of what our life with God will be on this earth. We would be less vulnerable, that is to say, less easily shattered by disillusionment and discouragement."

In classical spiritual language, the journey, the seeking, has been described in phases or stages.

> Christian life consists of intimate conversations with God in prayer, achieved through a threefold process: passing though the purgative, illuminative, and unitive ways successively. Discipline in life and prayer removes the obstacles and purges the senses, and so the soul moves to a second stage of Christian existence, in which the soul is progressively illumined by the gifts of God.

> And then there is entrance into a state of perfect
> mystical union with God in which the theological
> and moral virtues are practiced to a heroic degree.

In pre–Vatican II times, the tendency in Church circles was to assume that the mystical or unitive stage was for those men and women who were committed to contemplation in cloistered communities, and possibly some few chosen people who lived "in the world," but that the spirituality of the laity was basically formed through the purgative way addressing the need for conversion and forgiveness.

A new breath of the Spirit became apparent when Vatican II clarified that "all Christians in any state or walk of life are called to the fullness of Christian life and to the perfection of love, and by this holiness a more human manner of life is fostered also in earthly society" (Constitution on the Church, 40).

Spiritual writers continue to recognize that there are unfolding phases in the spiritual journey. Some wisely suggest that today, people may more readily identify with stages of certainty, searching, and intimacy. Some are quick to point out that these three phases are not necessarily sequential, that aspects of each phase may coexist at any point.

The certainty phase is characterized by a deference to a higher authority, the certainty that one experiences in following a well-defined system of rules. In this stage prayer and spiritual life are mainly formal and structured; prayer is a duty or even an obstacle course we must complete to get to God.

At some point, whether in adolescence or a midlife crisis, the security of certainty is challenged. We begin to question the source of our beliefs and our values. We may discover that some of our images and approaches to life are holdovers from an earlier time in life, sometimes linked with unresolved issues. It is a time of searching. The call is to persevere in the darkness as we begin to discover God in new ways even in the midst of the confusion.

As we are freed from the idea that we must earn love, and open to and transformed by the unconditional love of God, we come to a greater intimacy, an openness and honesty. We experience not only a greater self-awareness, but a tolerance and compassion for our own complexity, and for that of others. We surrender, unknowing, to the unknown. We allow ourselves to be focused on the love of God, revealed in Jesus, and to become channels of that love to others.

We *are* on a journey. Each of us has been invited to make that journey in the company of Jesus, who does indeed go before us, so that we can follow in his footsteps.

For your consideration and prayerful reflection:

- Using the threefold dynamic described above, how does your own journey reflect each of the phases?

- Read Luke 5:27–28. Imagine yourself as Levi, sitting at his desk. Imagine Jesus coming up to you, as he came to Levi, and saying, "Follow me." What are your feelings? Where do you resist? Where are you eager? See yourself rising up, leaving everything, and going with Jesus. Let your imagination flow as you see yourself with Jesus on your journey. Journal about your experience.

fifteen

Some Maps

"Follow me. . . . I am the Way."

—John 1:43; 14:6

No one, except a fool, sets out for a far place without seeking advice from those who have made the journey. We want to know about the seasons and the weather we can expect; we want to know the places that are inhabited, the places that may be dangerous for an inexperienced traveler. We want to be alerted to stops along the road where we can be refreshed, or visit some particularly significant place. We ask how we will know when we are nearing our destination, especially when the road branches off in many directions.

The journey home is in some respects as significant as the arrival there. Some one has wisely said that "all the way home is home since Jesus said that he is 'the way.'"

Clearly the way is given to us in the life and teachings of Jesus. The gospel holds for us a way of life that centers us clearly in the will of God.

Each of us must cut a path that, while gospel-centered, is shaped by our own particular personality, history, and gifts.

The Christian tradition offers any number of paths or models for following Christ. To speak of only a few, there are the ways of St. Francis of Assisi, and of St. Dominic, of Ignatius of Loyola, of the Carmelites John of the Cross and Teresa of Avila, and even the "little way" of Therese of Lisieux.

Each of these ways is an authentic approach to the living of the gospel, of arriving home at the center of one's existence. Each Christian is invited to seek the way that most resonates within him or her.

When one is serious about the path or career one has chosen, it is essential that one submit to the discipline inherent in that way. If one desires to be a nurse, one enters into a nursing program and follows what may seem like a rigidity in the specifics of nursery care and protocols. So, too, in any profession.

The same is true for those who are serious about inner spiritual transformation.

For religious, the novitiate or seminary has long provided a basic discipline of prayer, study, order of life, trusting that if the novice or seminarian submits to what is expected, he or she will emerge, not marked by the rigidity of the system, but rather freed to be the creative, original religious person that lies like seed in the center of each soul.

The same is largely true for those who enter a sacramental marriage. What is fostered is the fullness of a woman and a man as spouse, as parent, as a loving, generative person in the family and community.

In a society that is marked by compulsiveness, and has even been described as "addictive," many have found in Alcoholics Anonymous, founded in the 1930s, a program that has supported their journey into healing and sobriety. Richard Rohr suggests that the Twelve Step program may well be *the* contemporary American spirituality. The connection of the process of coming from the off-centeredness that fosters addiction, to one's true center is immediately apparent.

Whatever the program, whatever the path one chooses on the road toward wholeness and healing, it serves as a means of transformation. Each program or course is ideally structured to maximize the inner transformation of a person.

Such a process has parameters. Each demands discipline, generosity, obedience, and a readiness to die to the ego. One might use the image of the program being the cocoon phase of the caterpillar. Those with an attitude or intention of refusing the discipline or just getting by will wither and die, or be crippled, satisfied with the status quo, living the worst of the culture, with little energy and much apathy. Those who give themselves unreservedly to the expectations of the process are transformed beyond what is required.

As life unfolds, it is helpful to reflect on the paths we have taken, or along which we have been led. Since the journey continues to our final breath, we continue to make use of the maps that have been given to us.

For your consideration and prayerful reflection:

- What maps have helped shape your spiritual journey? Has the discipline called for by the way you have chosen been helpful to you? How well have you adhered to it?

- Who have been the people you trust as guides on your own inner journey? They may be living or they may be some holy person whose writings and spirit have mentored you.

sixteen

Staying on Course

*"Make your home in me, as I make
mine in you."*

—John 15:4

The incredible presence of God within us and ourselves
with God is almost too much to take in. We know, all too
well, that even with the best of intentions we slip away from
the center and focus of our lives. We come to the end of the
day wearied with the struggle, wondering what has sapped us
of energy, why our interactions have been less than satisfactory and perhaps even hurtful.

How do we maintain our centeredness; how do we respond to Christ's invitation to make our home in him?

Along with a commitment to daily prayer that brings us intentionally to the center of our souls where God dwells, there is a practice that can help us to stay on track. It is known as Examination of Consciousness or Awareness Exercise. It comes to us through St. Ignatius of Loyola, who recommended it to those for whom he was spiritual guide, assuring them that if one were faithful to its daily use, the practice would support them in times when because of travel or sickness or apostolic demands, it was difficult to find time for more extensive prayer.

At the end of the day, this exercise can provide a time to reflect on the day, to give thanks for what may not have been noticed as gift, and to make amends for failures, and to resume the journey.

Many will recall an earlier practice called the examination of conscience, made, usually at the end of the day. One reflected on the failures of the day, then made an act of contrition. Before retiring, one was made "right with God."

The renewal of this Ignatian tradition extends this practice to include what have been the gifts of the day, what is the deep desire of the heart, an awareness of how God has been calling one through the day, how one may have failed, and finally a prayer for the gift needed in the coming hours or day.

Marion Cowan suggests that these five steps correspond in some measure with five statements frequently used in a good human relationship: "Thank you," "Help me," "I love you," "Forgive me," "Be with me."

Altogether the practice is a matter of perhaps ten minutes. Some people have found it helpful to take the time at the end of the work day, perhaps as one is traveling home, since it seems at that time to pull together the day before entering into family time. Many people make this exercise a part of prayer at the close of the day.

Let us reflect briefly on each step.

1. Thank you. As we look back over the day, we recall what has been a gift. It is not enough to say a general "Thanks, God." Rather, one recalls specific moments that we now realize have been gifts of God, for example, a letter from a loved one, a beautiful sunrise, dew on a rose, a smile through tears in the eyes of a child, a successful meeting. For each gift, we thank God.

2. Help me. What is it that our hearts yearn for? Certainly we desire light and understanding to be able to follow Christ more closely, to know what God wants for us. But we can also name what our need is at this time, perhaps to know with greater certitude the love that God has for us, or for a deeper prayer. We name our need as we are aware of it, and we ask God's help.

3. I love you. How has God been inviting me during the day? Whether or not I responded, I need to be aware of those sometimes subtle "nudges of grace," for example: to say a kind and appreciative word to a fellow worker, to make a phone call to a friend who has been struggling, to put down one's pen when someone interrupts at work, to turn off the TV when a visitor comes, to bring a flower or small gift to a loved one, or even to pause for a moment of prayer. God has been calling; God was "knocking at the door."

4. Forgive me. If Jesus were to come to you as you are reflecting on your day and if he asked you, "For what do you want forgiveness and healing?" what would surface from the day? An unfriendly remark? Not taking time with a child who just wanted to be noticed? Overeating? In the awareness, one asks forgiveness, may pray for the person offended, and when appropriate, plans to make amends.

5. Be with me. Finally one asks for the gifts needed in the hours and in the day ahead. Often this part of this exercise grows out of the areas we have recognized as needing forgiveness and healing. So, if one has been impatient, one can ask that Christ would share his patience with us; if one has been unkind, one can ask for a share in the kindness and compassion of Christ.

The practice brings the day to closure and prepares for the coming day, so that we can rest peacefully and enter the new day with joy and gratitude.

For your consideration and prayerful reflection:

• You may find the following articulation of this exercise
  a help and guide as you bring your day to a close:

> Lord Jesus Christ,
> at the close of this day I come before you.
> Center my heart deep within your own;
> penetrate me with a growing awareness
> of your love and a greater desire to serve you.
>
> Lord Jesus, I thank you for the gifts of this day.
> . . .
>
> Lord Jesus, this is what I most need and desire
> from your goodness. . . .
>
> Lord Jesus, through this day you have been
> calling me and inviting me in these ways. . . .
>
> Lord Jesus, I ask for healing and forgiveness
> for the times today when I was less than faithful.
> . . .
>
> Lord Jesus be with me with your own gift of. . . .
>
> Lord Jesus, compassionate heart of God,
> as your disciple and in your Spirit, may my life
> be ever more given to the glory of God. Amen.

seventeen

In the Company of Mary

> *"Let what you have said be done to me."*

—Luke 1:38

These words of Mary are among the deepest sentiments of every Christian disciple. She shows us the way to hear, to accept, and then to proclaim the word of God. She is, as Raymond Brown writes, "the first and model disciple," well worth our own pondering as we consider how to live this vocational call to discipleship. When truly centered, we become, like Mary, a disciple of Jesus.

Mary opened herself to hearing the Word of God. Like a seed it dropped to the center of her being, and she received the Word without really knowing what it might mean for her life. But she faithfully embraced and pondered the mystery of God's presence within her.

Even before the Word is fully formed within her, she goes "in haste" to be with her cousin Elizabeth in her need. And the Christ within her ministers to the unborn John. What a consolation for us that even in and through our sometimes less than full discipleship, God can reach out and touch others.

Mary, first disciple, gives birth to the Christ in our world. She gives him eyes to see and ears to hear and hands to touch. So, too, as the Word of God takes root in the depths of our souls, we become his presence in our world, for as Saint Teresa reminds us, "Today, Christ has no body but ours, no hands to touch, no eyes to see, no ears to hear, no lips to speak, no feet to bring his message, except ours."

The words of the poet G. M. Hopkins in his poem "Margaret Clitheroe" apply to Mary, "she was a woman, upright, outright, /her will was bent to God." She lived in a world, not unlike our own, where tyranny reigned, the poor were oppressed, religious practice had lost its verve. In the midst of the chaos of her times, she walked with integrity.

At Cana, she is among the first to recognize the impending embarrassment of the newly married couple, and approaches Jesus, makes her request, and even after an apparent rebuff, she calmly tells the servants to "do whatever he tells you" (Jn 2:5).

When she is concerned about her son, she comes to see for herself if indeed, as she has heard, he has lost his mind.

At the foot of the cross she stands. The birth pangs of Bethlehem must have been as nothing to the painful ripping of her heart as she ponders her beloved son dying like a criminal. The Word that had formed within her womb, *formed her*, body and soul, into the faithful woman who endures.

In the Acts of the Apostles, we find Mary, after the Ascension, in the upper room when she gathered with the other disciples. With them, she received the Spirit. One might almost think that her presence drew the Spirit. The scene at the beginning of the Acts of the Apostles is reminiscent of the visit of the angel to Mary and the overshadowing by the Spirit at the beginning of the gospel of Luke.

The pentecostal Spirit is indeed the annunciation and conception of the post-resurrection community of the Church. Artists have loved to portray this event with Mary in the midst of the apostles. She is truly, as Vatican II claims her to be, "Mother of the Church."

Mary is the first disciple. She is model of what it means to live totally centered in God, and what it means to go with haste to our neighbor in need, what it means to ponder the mystery of life as it unfolds, what it means to stand firm in the midst of suffering in the conviction that for a follower of Jesus, it is death that leads to the fullness of life.

For your consideration and prayerful reflection:

- Use the words of Mary, "Be it done to me according to your Word," as a mantra, slowly repeating these words over and over.

- Write your own prayer of discipleship, asking for the grace to live totally centered in God, to stand firm in the midst of suffering, to reach out to those in need, and to ponder your own life as it continues to unfold in the mystery of God's immense love and faithfulness. Pray it often.

References

Chapter 3

Jean Houston, *The Search for the Beloved* (Los Angeles: Jeremy P. Tarcher, Inc., 1987).

Chapter 5

E. Allison Peers, Ed., "Spiritual Canticle," *The Complete Works of Saint John of the Cross* (London: Burns Oates, 1943), 33.

W.H. Gardner, Ed., *The Poems and Prose Gerard Manley Hopkins* (New York: Penguin Books, 1971).

Jessica Powers, *The Selected Poetry of Jessica Powers,* edited by Regina Siegfried and Robert F. Morneau (Washington: ICS Publications, 1999).

Thomas Merton, *Learning to Love* (San Francisco: HarperSanFrancisco, 1997), 235.

Chapter 6
Thomas Merton, *Conjectures of a Guilty Bystander* (Garden City, NY: Doubleday & Company, Inc., 1966), 140–42.

Chapter 7
Thomas Keating, *Open Mind, Open Heart* (New York: Continuum, 2006).

Chapter 8
Richard P. McBrien, *Catholicism* (San Francisco: Harper SanFrancisco, 1994), 787.

Chapter 10
Ilia Delio, *The Humility of God* (Cincinnati: St. Anthony Messenger Press, 2005), 29.
Louis M. Savary and Patricia H. Berne, *Kything, The Art of Spiritual Presence* (Mahwah, NJ: Paulist Press, 1988).

Chapter 13
Delio, 31.

Chapter 14
Caryll Houselander, *The Reed of God* (Notre Dame, IN: Christian Classics, 2006), 108.
McBrien, 1036.

Taken from "Opening to Love: A Paradigm for Growth in Relationship with God" by Briege O'Hare, 27–36, *Spiritual Direction*, Vol. 10, No. 2, June 2004.

Chapter 16

Marian Cowan, C.S.J., and John Carroll Futrell, S.J., *Companions in Grace: A Handbook for Directors of the Spiritual Exercises of St. Ignatius of Loyola* (Kansas City: Sheed and Ward, 1993), 35–37.

Chapter 17

Gardener, 78–79.

Raymond Brown, *A Coming Christ in Advent* (Collegeville, MN: The Liturgical Press, 1988), 60.

Marie Schwan, C.S.J., is a Sister of St. Joseph of Medaille, Louisiana. Schwan is perhaps best known for the five-book Take and Receive series that she wrote with Jacqueline Bergan. She is currently a spiritual director and retreat leader at the Sioux Spiritual Center in South Dakota. A teacher by profession, she has served in administration and formation in her congregation, and as associate director of Jesuit Retreat House in Oshkosh, Wisconsin.

Founded in 1865, Ave Maria Press,
a ministry of the Congregation of
Holy Cross, is a Catholic publishing
company that serves the spiritual and
formative needs of the Church and its
schools, institutions, and ministers;
Christian individuals and families; and
others seeking spiritual nourishment.

For a complete listing of titles from

Ave Maria Press

Sorin Books

Forest of Peace

Christian Classics

visit www.avemariapress.com

 ave maria press / Notre Dame, IN 46556
A Ministry of the Indiana Province of Holy Cross